DEEP *friendship*

DEEP
friendship
Moving Beyond the Superficial

FRANCISCO UGARTE

Scepter

This is an adapted translation of *El arte de la amistad*, copyright © 2014 Francisco Ugarte Corcuera, Ediciones Rialp, S.A., Madrid, Spain.

While every effort has been made to obtain existing accepted English translation or the English original of quoted text, some quotes have been translated by Scepter Publishers in the instance of no accepted English equivalent having been found.

English translation, copyright © 2016 by Scepter Publishers, Inc.
Published by Scepter Publishers, Inc.
info@scepterpublishers.org
www.scepterpublishers.org
800-322-8773
New York

Text and cover by Rose Design

Printed in the United States of America

Library of Congress Cataloging-in-Publication Data

Names: Ugarte Corcuera, Francisco, author.
Title: Deep friendship : moving beyond the superficial / Francisco Ugarte.
Other titles: Arte de la amistad. English
Description: New York : Scepter Publishers, 2016.
Identifiers: LCCN 2016049253 (print) | LCCN 2016049772 (ebook) | ISBN 9781594172649 (pbk. : alk. paper) | ISBN 9781594172656
Subjects: LCSH: Friendship.
Classification: LCC BJ1533.F8 U3313 2016 (print) | LCC BJ1533.F8 (ebook) | DDC 177/.62—dc23
LC record available at https://lccn.loc.gov/2016049253

ISBN book 978-1-59417-264-9
ebook 978-1-59417-265-6

Contents

Introduction

How many real friends does a person usually have? Not "friends" in the sense of mere "acquaintances," but *real friends*? Perhaps in trying to answer this question, each of us will first think of our own situations: "How many real friends do *I* have?" For many, the answer might be troubling, especially if we understand the importance of and need for friendship. Those who lack real friends find themselves tremendously limited in many facets of life, because we all need friends to complement ourselves: in the material and in the spiritual, in the intellectual and in the emotional, in work and in relaxation. Without friends, we experience loneliness, insecurity, and boredom. True friendship is one of our greatest personal treasures.

This leads us to another question: Is it easy or difficult to make a good friend? We recognize that some individuals, although ordinarily in contact with a great number of people for different reasons, don't have friends. Why? The answer is an apparent paradox. On one hand, we see that friendship is something very natural, and it seems that anyone could obtain it. But experience tends to show us the opposite, leading us to conclude that true friendship is difficult to establish. Plutarch thought that "a steadfast friend is something rare and hard to find."[1] The causes of this can be quite different for many reasons, among them: a temperament lacking in empathy, distrust of others, egoistic individualism, busy lifestyles and lack of time, superficiality in human relationships, and a lack of openness to the ideas or habits of others. It may also happen that we do not understand what makes up real friendship and, consequently, do not know how to go about behaving as friends. For that reason, it is useful to begin by resolving this last difficulty. If we attain a clear idea of what friendship is, then we can solve the other problems with greater ease, as we will know what path to follow and what obstacles to overcome in order to make—and be—true friends.

---

1. Plutarch, *Moralia II*, trans. Frank Cole Babbitt, (Cambridge, MA: Harvard University Press, 1971), p. 69.

In this present work, after pointing out the value of friendship through citation of authors of different time periods, I will make an analysis that will enable us to understand what friendship is—and what are the factors or elements which make it up. If we start from the basis that each friendship is an affective relationship between two or more persons who understand each other, share interests, and help each other in an unconditional way, it will be clear why the order of the chapters is as follows:

First, the value of friendship; second, emotional affinity, which consists in the communication of feelings and is necessary for personal closeness between individuals; third, understanding our friends—that is to say, having mutual knowledge of each other, supported by affection; fourth, common interests, which constitute the objective content of the friendship, since without them, the relationship would be empty; fifth, and at a deeper level, an interest in our friends, which is equivalent to effective love and which translates into a real desire that our friends attain the good that is proper to them— their true happiness.

1.

The Value of Friendship

The general view of the value of friendship—in itself and for the life of any particular person—seems to be unanimous. Nearly everyone agrees on its importance and its many benefits. The value of friendship does not have to be demonstrated because it shows itself in an obvious way, whether we've had the experience of enjoying what friends represent or we feel the need for them. In this second case, there may not be a direct understanding of friendship, but we can evaluate it by the emptiness produced by its absence.

Sublime things have been said throughout history on the need for friendship, expressing the general conviction of how necessary it is to human life to be able to count on friends. The Bible's Book of Sirach says:

> A faithful friend is a sturdy shelter:
> he that has found one has found a treasure.
> There is nothing so precious as a faithful friend,
> and no scales can measure his excellence. (Sir 6:14–15)

It's significant that a friend is compared to a treasure of incalculable value, because certainly what a friend provides is something of much greater value than any material object, including money. And some authors have shown how much they appreciate friendship, considering it not only one of the highest goods but the greatest of all. Aristotle noted that "we hold that a friend is one of the greatest goods."[1] Cicero, referring to friendship, expressed it as follows: "With the exception of wisdom, I am inclined to think nothing better than this has been given to man by the immortal gods."[2] Ortega y Gasset held that "a delicately chiseled friendship, cared

---

1. Aristotle, *The Eudemian Ethics*, trans. Brad Inwood and Raphael Woolf, (New York: Cambridge University Press, 2013), VII 1234b, p. 121.

2. Marcus Tullius Cicero, *On Old Age, On Friendship, and On Divination*, trans. W. A. Falconer (Cambridge, MA: Harvard University Press, 1923).

for as one cares for a work of art, is the summit of the universe. "[3]

It is also interesting to point out that the value of friendship is recognized spontaneously by persons of all ages, including children, as the following example demonstrates. It concerns a widely reported survey, organized by the Psychology Department of the University of Louvain in Belgium. A group of children below the age of twelve were given three drawings depicting three different ways of celebrating a birthday. In the first, there appeared only the child, surrounded by a great number of presents; in the second, the child was seated at table with his parents and on the table was a large package containing a gift; in the third, there was no present, but the child was accompanied by many people, all of his family and a great number of friends. The question was very simple: In which of these three ways do you prefer to celebrate your birthday?

The response was as follows: The first two ways barely got fifteen percent each, while the third easily exceeded sixty percent. The survey

---

3. José Ortega y Gasset, *Obras completas II: El Espectador*, (Madrid: Revista de Occidente, 1946), p. 511.

was later repeated many times and in very different places, and the results were always the same.[4]

What is the reason for this general recognition of friendship? In what is its value rooted? Without attempting to go into all of the reasons why friendship is such a great good, I will share several.

Friendship Increases Joy and Mitigates Suffering

When we feel happy because of some favorable event in our lives or for some good that we have received, we tend to share it with the persons whom we love. When we do so, we note how that joy intensifies within us. When the joy is shared with others, it is not only not lost—as might happen with material things— but it increases. And, in contrast to this, when sufferings occur, it is the opposite. On sharing them with our friends, their depressing effect is reduced; we experience relief because we no longer have to bear them alone. For this reason, Francis Bacon said that friendship "redoubleth

---

4. See Jose Maria Cabodevilla, *El cielo en palabras terrenas*, (Madrid: Paulinas, 1990), p. 161.

joys, and cutteth griefs in halves."[5] Santiago Ramón y Cajal stressed that the joviality of friends constitutes the best antidote to the disappointments of the world and the fatigues of work.[6] And Felipe Jacinto Sala expressed in poetic terms the benefit of sharing one's sufferings with a friend: "The soul feels misty and sad while oppressed by secret sorrows. But if communicated to a faithful friend, one is relieved of the weight of one's torment."[7]

Friendship Does Away with Loneliness

Some people are habitually surrounded by many people and, in spite of that, feel alone because they lack relationships of friendship. This means that the problem of loneliness does not depend so much on the physical proximity of people but on the lack of interior bonds with

---

5. Francis Bacon, "Of Friendship," *The Essays: Or Counsels Civil and Moral*, (New York: Oxford University Press, 1999), p. 62.

6. Santiago Ramón y Cajal, Charlas de café: pensamientos, anécdotas y confidencias, (Madrid: Espasa-Calpe 1966), p. 24.

7. Felipe Jacinto Sala, "La nube," *Nuevas fabulas*, (Barcelona: Librería de Juan y Antonio Bastinos, 1886), p. 59.

them. This can occur when there is no friendship with the persons with whom we live, with the consequent suffering that accompanies it. For this reason, Aristotle says that "friendlessness and isolation are most dreadful, since our whole life and our voluntary associations are bound up with friends."[8] And Francis Bacon expresses forcefully that "it is a mere and miserable solitude to want true friends; without which the world is but a wilderness; and even in this sense also of solitude, whosoever in the frame of his nature and affections, is unfit for friendship, he taketh it of the beast, and not from humanity."[9] In contrast, the relationship of friendship leads us to be one with our friends, which demands being close to them and helping them not to feel lonely, because, as St. Thomas Aquinas said, when a person "loves another with the love of friendship, he wills good to him, just as he wills good to himself. Hence a friend is called a man's 'other self.'"[10]

---

8. Aristotle, *Eudemian Ethics*, VII.1.5, 1235a, p. 121.

9. Bacon, "Of Friendship," p. 60.

10. Thomas Aquinas, *Summa Theologica*, 1–2, q. 28, a. 1, trans. Fathers of the English Dominican Province, (New York: Benziger Bros., 1948).

Friendship Transforms Negative Feelings

When a friendship is real, the perception of the friend and of all that refers to him or her becomes surprisingly positive, because of the affection that we feel. Any incidence of conflict becomes an occasion of union; what in other cases produces the bitter effect of envy becomes a source of joy, because the good of our friend is considered as our own. This is what we read with respect to the relationship of St. Gregory Nazianzen and St. Basil the Great, two close friends of the fourth century. Here is what St. Gregory said: "We were impelled by equal hopes, in a pursuit especially obnoxious to envy, that of letters. Yet envy we knew not, and emulation was of service to us. We struggled, not each to gain the first place for himself, but to yield it to the other; for we made each other's reputation to be our own."[11] This is the wonderful thing about true friendship: each of us experiences a true joy in the face of triumphs and

---

11. Gregory Nazianzen, "Sermon 43: The Panegyric on S. Basil," in *Nicene and Post-Nicene Fathers, Second Series VII*, trans. Charles Gordon Browne and James Edward Swallow, ed. Philip Schaff and Rev. Henry Wallace (New York: Cosimo, 2007), p. 402.

anything else that is good for our friend, something that is not the case when a friendship is not true. For this reason, Oscar Wilde affirmed quite rightly that "anybody can sympathize with the sufferings of a friend, but it requires a very fine nature . . . to sympathize with a friend's success."[12]

Friendship Protects and Is a Support in Difficulties

"A faithful friend is a sturdy shelter; he that has found one has found a treasure" (Sir 6:14), the sacred author assures us, because if our friend is really faithful, that person's support is always unconditional; a friend knows how to stick with us in all circumstances, in the good and in the bad.

"It's easy enough . . . being loyal to one's friend when they're in the right; the hard thing is when they're behaving badly,"[13] said André Malraux. As an authentic friend, we each give priority to our friend over ourselves; we are

---

12. Oscar Wilde, *The Soul of Man under Socialism*, (New York: Max N. Maisel, 1915), p. 57.

13. André Malraux, *Man's Hope*, trans. Stuart Gilbert and Alastair Macdonald, (New York: Random House, 1938), p. 265.

ready to leave aside our likes and interests if the needs of our friend require this. This is shown especially in difficult situations which require us to renounce ourselves or to run risks,—or when it is necessary to support the other person. It is also in those adverse circumstances that we discover a false friendship, as the following fable of Aesop expresses graphically:

> Two fellows were travelling together through a wood, when a Bear rushed out upon them. One of the travelers happened to be in front, and he seized hold of the branch of a tree, and hid himself among the leaves. The other, seeing no help for it, threw himself flat down upon the ground, with his face in the dust. The Bear, coming up to him, put his muzzle close to his ear, and sniffed and sniffed. But at last with a growl he shook his head and slouched off, for bears will not touch dead meat. Then the fellow in the tree came down to his comrade, and, laughing, said "What was it that Master Bruin whispered to you?"
>
> "He told me," said the other, "Never Trust a Friend Who Deserts You At A Pinch."[14]

---

14. Aesop, "The Two Fellows and the Bear," *Aesop's Fables*, retold by Joseph Jacobs, 1902. This text is in the public domain.

Friendship Is Disinterested and Accompanies Us to the End

The disinterest in friendship refers to our own interests—putting our own interests in second place and permitting those of our friend to prevail. The interest in our friend should also be total and without limits, even when it is a matter of risking our own lives. The following dialogue between a soldier and his commander, during a battle, reflects this eloquently:

> The soldier: "My friend has not returned from the field of battle, sir, and I request permission to go and look for him."
>
> The commander: "Permission denied. I don't want you to risk your life for a man who is probably dead."
>
> The soldier, ignoring the prohibition, left, and an hour later returned, mortally wounded, but carrying the body of his friend. The commander was furious: "I told you he was dead! Now I've lost two men! Tell me, was it worthwhile going out to bring back a cadaver?"
>
> The dying soldier answered, "Of course, it was, sir! When I found him, he was still alive and he was able to tell me: 'Jaime, I was sure that you would come.'"

Another event, from classical times, underlines the value of friendship until death, and at the same time, it produced a real transformation in someone who was planning to end a man's life. They say that when the Pythagorean philosopher Phintias was condemned to death by the despot Dionysius, he asked for a one-day permission to go to his house, outside of the city, to put his affairs in order. Dionysius consented on the condition that Phintias leave with him his friend Damon as a hostage. When Dionysius saw the friend present himself confidently and then saw Phintias return on time, instead of having him executed, Dionysius humbly asked to be admitted to the friendship of both, which had moved him so deeply.[15]

Friendship Promotes and Increases Happiness

To what extent can friends help in the attainment of the happiness for which every human being yearns? Aristotle asked himself whether friendship is or is not necessary for happiness, after

---

15. Kitty Ferguson, *Pythagoras: His Lives and the Legacy of a Rational Universe*, (Electronic Edition: London: Icon Books, 2010; Print Edition: New York: Walker, 2008).

affirming that happiness consists in virtue—
and more specifically, in contemplative virtue
(which confers on the wise a kind of self-suf-
ficiency that seems to eliminate the need for
anything else to be happy). In his answer he set
aside speculative analysis and fixed on the exis-
tential experience, from which he concluded
that it is clearly better to spend one's days with
friends and virtuous persons than with strangers
and whoever happens to show up. The happy
person, therefore, needs to have friends.[16]

In today's scientific literature, there are
many studies that confirm the close influence
of friendship on happiness. As the psychologist
Melikşah Demir notes, "decades of empirical
research have shown that having friends and
experiences of close friendship . . . are essential predictors of happiness . . . which shows
that the role of friendships in happiness has
been called 'the deep truth.'"[17] It ranks above
other factors such as physical health, profes-
sional success, and well-being, which can also

---

16. See Aristotle, *Nicomachean Ethics*, IX, 9, 1169b 7.

17. Melikşah Demir, Ayça Özen, Aysun Dogan, Nicholas A. Bilyk, and Finita A. Tyrell, "I Matter to My Friend, Therefore I am Happy: Friendship, Mattering, and Happiness," *Journal of Happiness Studies* 12, no. 6 (December 2011): pp. 983–1005.

contribute to people being happier but with less influence than friendship.

From another point of view, if happiness derives from the plenitude that we attain when we put into play all of our capabilities and develop our strengths,[18] we should keep in mind that we cannot dispense with friendship if we want to attain this plenitude, as it is a necessary factor for human perfecting. People cannot develop themselves alone; in order to grow and improve, they must have friends. Therefore, we could say that friendship is not something added to happiness but is an integral element of it, since without friendship, human perfection remains incomplete, and without this, happiness would not be possible.[19]

Friendship Leads to Union with God

A sure indicator of true friendship is that we desire the improvement and continual advancement of our friend and use the means at our

---

18. See Francisco Ugarte, *From Resentment to Forgiveness: A Gateway to Happiness* (New York: Scepter, 2008).

19. See Antonio Malo, *Antropología de la afectividad* (Pamplona: EUNSA, 2004), p. 115.

disposal to help him or her to attain this. True friends offer each other the best of themselves, all with the sole desire of favoring each other. For people of faith, there is no doubt as to the supreme good that we can offer our friends, which is to lead them toward God, as Fernando Ocáriz points out accurately. "Since love leads one to desire and procure the good for the one that one loves, the order of charity leads one chiefly to procure the union of the other with God, for in this is the greatest good, the definitive."[20] And how do we concretize this action? Pope Francis gives the answer when he explains, "In this preaching, which is always respectful and gentle, the first step is personal dialogue, when the other person speaks and shares his or her joys, hopes and concerns for loved ones, or so many other heartfelt needs. Only afterwards is it possible to bring up God's word . . . always keeping in mind the fundamental message: the personal love of God who became man, who gave himself up for us, who is living and who offers us his salvation and his friendship. . . ."[21]

---

20. Fernando Ocáriz, *Amar Con Obras: a Dios y a los hombres*, (Madrid: Palabra, 1974), p. 103.

21. Pope Francis, Apostolic exhortation *Evangelii Gaudium* (November 2013), p. 128.

Although the value of friendship shows itself in a very obvious way and therefore does not need to be demonstrated, the motives pointed out here confirm that friendship is a true treasure worth cultivating and explain why agreement about the value of friendship is practically unanimous.

2.

Emotional Affinity (Bonding)

The Initial Meeting

Friendship is a process. Therefore, before considering the first element that constitutes it, it's worthwhile describing the steps that starting a friendship usually follow. In ordinary life, it is normal to have relationships with many people for various motives—such as those related to family, work, socializing, religion, and sports—and in the majority of cases, bonds of friendship are not established. Nevertheless, these personal relationships are always the point of departure for developing a friendship. Those initial encounters with others can be by chance or intentional. The first are the most frequent and natural. As a consequence of activities we carry out, we all meet others, until then unknown to us. In other cases, we set out with the express intention of getting to know others—as is the case when we join social or sports clubs in order to develop relationships. This also happens when we seek opportunities to enter into contact with particular persons, whom until that moment, we had only heard about. In all of these cases, the possibility of friendship is open, but only to a point. To reach it, it is necessary to take various steps, climb different stairs.

Companionship

If the initial encounter continues, through conversation and interaction, we and the prospective friend begin to get to know each other. For example, if we work together, we will each notice aspects of the other, so that little by little, we stop being strangers. We establish a relationship between ourselves, the content of which is based on the activities we carry out in common and on the incipient knowledge that we have of each other up till that moment. This relationship can be called companionship. Companions are, for example, the students in the same classroom, the members of a football team, the employees in a factory, the associates in a company, and the members of a religious organization. Their bonds are weak and depend heavily on the motive that unites them—the activity that they carry out together—so that if this were lacking, they would stop seeing one another. The student who changes schools loses old companions, the athlete who leaves the team doesn't see those with whom he or she used to play, one who changes jobs loses the relationship with former colleagues, and so on. Each of these cases reflects the point at which the relationship of companionship might be weak.

The principal weakness of companionship is rooted in the lack of personal content in the relationship. The person of the companion becomes a simple circumstance of what we are fundamentally seeking: the activity that we carry out in common. This situation can last a long time, as in the case of our working beside a colleague for years and not establishing a properly personal relationship with that person because we do not have access to his or her private life. Little interest in the person is, therefore, characteristic of simple fellowship.

Subjective and Objective Affinity

In contrast, at times it occurs that between two or more companions, there suddenly arises a desire for a closer relationship. This is due to the discovery of the affinity that exists between them, from which there arises the inclination to become closer. Until this point, we cannot yet speak of friendship, but we can intuit that companionship is going to be *the matrix*, the origin of friendship, insofar as the friends have always been companions in some sense previously. What is the affinity that produces the impulse to move from companionship to friendship? Affinity in the abstract refers to the similarity of one thing with another, a coinciding in some aspect. When it is a matter of affinity between persons, this similarity or coinciding can be on two levels, *subjective and objective*, which we will now examine.

The writer Jaime Balmes used to describe the qualities of the principal faculties of the human person in the following words: "a head of ice, arms of iron, a heart of fire,"[1] meaning that the intellect has to think with coolness and

---

1. Carlos Llano, *Humildad y liderazgo: ¿necesita el empresario ser humilde?* (Mexico City: Ediciones Ruz, 2004), p. 265.

objectivity, the will possess a strength capable of making important decisions and carrying them into practice, and the affectivity capable of becoming passionate with the intensity proper to feelings that are accurately focused. This third aspect, the subject of the present chapter, plays an essential role in friendship, since it is "in the sphere of affection, in the heart, where the most individual treasures of the life of a person are stored, where one pronounces one's most intimate word."[2] For that reason, "the emotions constitute our most personal and particular nucleus, much more so than our way of conducting ourselves or the range of our knowledge."[3]

When between two or more people there arises, spontaneously, a coinciding of affections, an emotional *in tune-ness*, which makes them experience the same feelings, we can say that there is between them an *affective* (*emotional*) *affinity* (*bonding*). This phenomenon is also usually referred to [in Spanish] as *simpatía*, which etymologically means "to feel with" the other

2. Dietrich von Hildebrand, *The Heart: An Analysis of Human and Divine Affectivity* (South Bend, IN: St. Augustine Press, 2007).

3. José Antonio Marina, *El laberinto sentimental*, (Barcelona: Anagrama, 1997), pp. 229–230.

person, to feel in unison. In English we would probably use like-minded or congenial. Friendships, in most cases, have as their starting point this congeniality. Yet other friendships not only do not begin with this initial congeniality but may even have to overcome an initial antipathy.

There are those who have a special facility to "empathize" with others from the first moments of their relationships because of their capacity to capture and transmit feelings. This quality makes them agreeable and helps them to make a good impression on those they deal with. Thus the relationships are facilitated and acquire that personal character from the outset. In general women, often possessing a more affective character, tend to enjoy this quality more than men. However, there are also negative feelings that produce a distancing and antipathy between persons, and women, due to an often greater weight of emotion, may experience these inclinations more intensely. A study cited by Goleman,[4] and carried out with 264 couples, concluded that the most important thing for women was to have "good communication."

---

4. Daniel Goleman, *Emotional Intelligence* (New York: Bantam, 1995), p. 132.

Meanwhile, the men complained that they wanted to carry out activities with their wives and that, instead, the response they frequently received was that the only thing that the women wanted to do was to talk. And the fact is that conversation is a privileged vehicle for the communication of feelings that sometimes presents itself as an urgent need.

Communication of Feelings and Getting Along Together

When subjective affinity awakens among those who were maintaining a relationship of simple companionship—when they notice signs of friendship—they experience a change. There is a spontaneous and reciprocal attraction, they enjoy each other's company, and their relationship flows naturally. Communication is favored and not only carried out through words but also by means of body language. A gesture, a look, or an attitude can say more than words because each is a vehicle for the transmission of feelings. Although it might seem an exaggeration, according to Goleman himself, the experts assure us that 90 percent or more of an emotional message is nonverbal.

This reciprocal attraction also favors personal contact. The developing friends seek occasions to be together, affection increases, their dealings become easier, and everything points, little by little, toward unity and mutual identification, which forms an essential part of friendship. This affective affinity, with its consequent communication of feelings, plays an important role in their dealings with one another, because "people call someone a friend who has close contact with another (the first characteristic), has the same tastes (the second), and shares sorrows and joys (the third)."[5]

Thus, when the affective (emotional) harmony is present, it produces a strong understanding among those so related, such that words can seem superfluous among them. Erasmus notes that true friendship has arrived when silence between the two parties seems agreeable. And vice versa, if one is careless about contact, the relationship declines because "brambles cover the path of friendship when one does not travel on it frequently,"[6] in the words of Antoine Rivarol.

---

5. Thomas Aquinas, "Lecture 4: The Acts or Effects of Friendship," *Commentary on The Nicomachean Ethics*, Book 9, no. 1800.

6. Antoine de Rivarol, *Pensamientos y Rivarolianas*, (Madrid: Editorial Perifica, 2006).

The Power of Affection

Affection that proceeds from feelings is distinguished from the love of the will, of which I will speak more later. Thomas Aquinas, to explain the power of sentimental love, affirms that people love for this reason "when a man does not know how to live without the one that he loves,"[7] and adds that "from two, friendship makes one by means of affection." Ortega, alluding to this same type of love, says that to love a person "is to be eager that he or she exists; not to admit, in what depends on oneself, the possibility of a universe where that person is absent."[8] It is a matter therefore, of a force which is oriented toward union, toward identification with the persons loved, who become an inseparable part of our own lives. Therefore, we call for and demand their presence. In analyzing, at the proper time, the role of the will in friendship, we have to take into account that such love can be notably strengthened by affective and emotional love. "Given that the human

7. Thomas Aquinas, *Commentary on Saint Matthew's Gospel*, 22, 4.

8. José Ortega y Gasset, "Estudios sobre el amor," in *Revista de Occidente*, (Madrid: Alianza Editorial, 1981), pp. 20–21.

person is not only a soul, nor isolated sensibility, the emotional has its place, its role, in the birth, the consolidation, and the expansive growth of love between people."[9]

Notice also that, when there is affinity between persons, communication of feelings benefits, moreover, the same feelings. For example, joy increases when we communicate it to others, and consolation makes sorrow more bearable. Nevertheless, for friendship to benefit from feelings, it is necessary that the feelings be "objective." There must be a due proportion between the stimulus proceeding from objects and the reactions awakened by them, in a way analogous to what happens in the order of intelligence, as von Hildebrand explains: "An act of knowing is objective when it captures the true nature of the object. And an affective response is objective when it corresponds to the value of the object."[10] This has to do as much with the quality as with the intensity of the reactions. If we rejoice at the unexpected news of the death of a friend, it is evident that the reaction is not objective,

9. Tomás Melendo, *Ocho lecciones sobre el amor humano*, (Madrid: Rialp, 1993), p. 101.

10. von Hildebrand, *La affectividad cristiana*, p. 98.

because the normal response in this case would be to become sad. Also, if we react with rage at someone who contradicts us in a matter of small importance, our reaction is not objective because it is not proportional to the stimulus that provoked it. "Objectivity" is a sign of affective maturity, that the feelings are well-formed, which is very important in relation to friendship.

In conclusion, we might say that affective affinity—supposing the maturity of the affectivity—plays an essential role in friendship, because it provides the relation between the subjects with its personal, intimate character, which mere companionship lacks.

The Weakness of Subjective Affinity

Nevertheless, after having underlined the importance of "liking" for friendship, we have to emphasize that this is not enough. Its weakness is rooted in the fact that affective affinity, that of the feelings, does not in itself offer sufficient guarantees that the relationship will acquire solidity and consistency. If a relationship is based exclusively on shared feelings, it will be subject to the changeability of those emotions and it will lack the support of the will. The following dialogue reflects how affection, when it has diminished, needs the will to arise again.

> "[Stephen,] My wife and I just don't have the same feelings for each other we used to have. I guess I just don't love her anymore and she doesn't love me. What can I do?"
>
> "The feeling isn't there anymore?" I asked.
>
> "That's right," he reaffirmed. "And we have three children we're really concerned about. What do you suggest?"
>
> "Love her," I replied.
>
> "I told you, the feeling just isn't there anymore."
>
> "Love her."
>
> "You don't understand. The feeling of love just isn't there."
>
> "Then love her. If the feeling isn't there, that's a good reason to love her."
>
> "But how do you love when you don't love?"
>
> "My friend, love is a verb. Love—the feeling—is a fruit of love, the verb. So love her. Serve her. Sacrifice. Listen to her. Empathize. Appreciate. Affirm her. Are you willing to do that?"[11]

---

11. Stephen R. Covey, *The 7 Habits of Highly Effective People: Powerful Lessons in Personal Change* (New York: Simon & Schuster,

The same thing can happen in the relationship of friendship. Affection can decay and require the support of the will, seeking to interrelate with the friend and thus reconstruct the relationship that has cooled off.

If a friendship has no content other than feelings, it can become deformed since affectivity, left to its own spontaneity, tends to turn in on itself in an egocentric way. And in this case, we would no longer see the friend as the terminus of affection, but rather seek in the relationship a personal and egoistic satisfaction—to feel ourselves liked, attended to, preferred. This could also lead us to adopt a possessive attitude toward our friend and to even experience jealousy if that person's friendship is shared with others, when "true friendship," as Lewis says, "is the least jealous of loves,"[12] This phenomenon of possessive friendship is usually frequent among adolescents, because they have not yet attained affective maturity.

---

12. C.S. Lewis, *The Four Loves*, (New York: Harcourt Brace, 1960), p. 61. "True Friendship is the least jealous of loves. Two friends delight to be joined by a third, and three by a fourth, if only the newcomer is qualified to become a real friend. They can then say, as the blessed souls say in Dante, 'Here comes one who will augment our loves.' For in this love 'to divide is not to take away.'"

Friendship, finally, requires content other than feelings. The affective affinity is like a lubricant used to help the pieces of a motor function easily and without friction. When a motor lacks oil, it usually becomes damaged or stops working. If, in human relationships, there is no empathy, if there is not that communication of feelings, which so greatly favors personal closeness, it is difficult to go beyond companionship. But what good is the lubricant if the motor lacks some pieces? The pieces are the *objective* content of the relationship, which will be analyzed later. First it is necessary to consider the intervention of *knowledge* in friendship, because without knowledge, affective affinity cannot arise. In what does knowing—understanding—a person deeply consist? This will be the subject of the next chapter.

3.

Understanding Our Friends

Human relationships are usually based on a superficial knowledge of other people, because we first know others in only their most exterior aspects: how they appear physically, how they speak, and how they behave socially. So there is the risk of principally focusing on appearance. This is due in good measure to the perspective and the attitude with which we see them from a distance, from the outside, as if we were dealing with and relating to mere objects. We can lose sight of the fact that they are "subjects"—persons who possess an interiority. As long as we do not see them from their most intimate selves—"from within outwards," relating their exterior selves to the roots from which they proceed—we do not really know them. If this occurs between those who consider themselves friends, we have to have doubts about their friendship, because for friendship to occur between two people, they must truly get to know each other.

Knowing a person deeply, how that person really is in his or her own individuality and singularity, means to *understand him or her*. And this understanding is indispensable for friendship, both in its process of gestation, where ordinarily the affective affinity takes place, and in its perfectioning, as I will detail later. For this reason, understanding is the second element of friendship, since it is an indispensable condition for relating adequately. In what does this understanding consist?

To understand our friends means to know and understand their interiority, to have access to their intimacy, to capture from within how each person really is. Is this possible? What is the path that we should follow? Although the answers are valid for interpersonal relationships in general, they apply in an especially appropriate way to the relationship of friendship.

Putting Ourselves in Another's Place

The first thing is not to lose sight of what we have already said: that we are facing dynamic "subjects" who have lives of their own, thoughts of their own, and personal ways of acting. We are not facing "static objects," which are classified according to pre-established criteria. This requires *putting ourselves in their shoes* in order to know them from themselves. And this putting ourselves in their shoes, in a profound and complete way, includes two levels: the emotional or affective, which contains our feelings, and the intellectual, made up of the other people's concepts and ways of thinking. We will analyze these separately, although in practice they are intermixed, because the human person is a unity.

Empathy

The capacity to put ourselves in another's place emotionally is called *empathy*.[1] Empathy is not the same as "*simpatía*." To sympathize—to have

---

1. Covey, *The 7 Habits of Highly Effective People*.

"*simpatico*"—as we have seen, means to "feel with" someone, to coincide affectively or sentimentally with another person, to feel in unison. Empathy, on the other hand, means "to feel within," for which it is necessary to "enter into another's feelings," or better yet, see to it that "the other enter into me" so that I feel what that person feels and thus understand him or her. In the words of Carlos Llano: "Empathy, which in Greek means to *feel within* (a difference from the word sympathy, that in Greek means to *feel with*), has become part of modern anthropology, thanks to the German existentialist philosopher (and medical doctor) Karl Jaspers. Jaspers' idea was that it was not enough for the doctor to have an intellectual representation of what the patient was suffering objectively and subjectively. He had to go beyond this to try to *feel interiorly* the same thing as the sick person was feeling."[2] According to this, when we begin to *empathize* with the other person, we begin to know that person's most profound individuality, therefore, *to understand* the friend on the affective or emotional level.

---

2. Carlos Llano, *El Liderazgo Anamórfico*, (Mexico City: IPADE, 1994). This is a technical note.

There are people who have this quality of empathy very deeply rooted, which makes it easy for others to identify with them from the very beginning. They entrust themselves intimately when they hardly know others because they *feel* themselves to be understood. They seek others out without expecting from them any practical or effective solution to the problems that they present; it is enough to *feel* their understanding, which they experience because these empathizers know how to put themselves into the place of the others and thus share their feelings or emotions. From this there arises a sincere affection—an affective affinity—that favors in a significant way the relationship of friendship.

Intellectual Understanding

The other necessary level for understanding to be complete is of an intellectual order. It consists in seeing the world as other people see it, understanding each person's conceptions or "paradigms." In this respect, Covey explains that "the word *paradigm* comes from the Greek. It was originally a scientific term and is more commonly used today to mean a model, theory, perception, assumption, or frame of reference,

In the more general sense, it is the way we 'see' the world—not in terms of our visual sense of sight, but in terms of perceiving, understanding, interpreting."[3] And he adds that "a paradigm is like a pair of glasses: it affects the way that you see everything in your life."[4] From our paradigms there come our attitudes and conduct.

A frequent error is to see others, interpret their attitudes, and judge their behavior from *our* paradigms, which in so many cases can be mistaken because of preconceived judgments or, in short, by our prejudices. This provokes a failure to understand others, because they are being seen "from without," that is to say, from ourselves. True understanding requires entering into the others intellectually, that is, understanding *their* paradigms, putting on their glasses to see reality as they see it and thus to understand what is in their interior worlds. From this perspective, we can also understand what blossoms forth from those intimate cells, their attitudes and their behaviors. When this occurs, friendship flows rapidly and leads to unity between the friends.

---

3. Covey, *The 7 Habits of Highly Effective People*, p. 23.
4. Covey, *The 7 Habits of Highly Effective People*, p. 121.

To attain what has just been described, it is not necessary *to agree* with the way of thinking of others. Stepping into their shoes, in order to see the world as they see it, does not signify accepting those visions, which sometimes could seem wrong to us, incomplete, partial, or whatever. What is important is that, on a basis of respect for the people with whom we are in contact, we know how to take off our own glasses for a moment and put on theirs, in order to get into their worlds. This is indispensable in regard to being friends. St. Josemaría Escrivá points out that "true friendship also means making a heartfelt effort to understand the convictions of our friends, even though we may never come to share them or accept them."[5]

These considerations are sufficient to conclude the importance of understanding at the two levels, emotional and intellectual. Empathy permits us to know others in their deepest individuality, at the most intimate level. Intellectual understanding makes it possible to grasp the others with profundity, to understand why they see things the way they see them. In both cases, it is a matter of acknowledging others' perspectives, of getting inside of them or letting them

---

5. Josemaría Escrivá, *Furrow* (New York: Scepter, 2011), p. 746.

get inside of us, in order to feel what they feel and understand what they understand.

Love, the Foundation of Understanding

This process, which leads to deep understanding, could leave the impression that it is a matter of a *technical nature*, which is resolved via a formula of action. Nothing is further from the reality. The foundation by which it is possible to understand a person deeply is a matter of love. And this is true for two reasons. The first is because the effort to place ourselves habitually in the shoes of others demands self-giving, renunciation of ourselves. This renunciation is only possible if there is an interior impulse, which proceeds from love, to maintain ourselves in this direction. When there is no love, we revert to our own selves, fall into egoism, and become incapable of "entering into the other" and thus understanding other people. Love is essential for friendship, as we will see further on, and one of its most important consequences is that it makes it possible to understand our friends.

The second reason—which requires broader development—is that in order to "enter" into another person, we need to develop a certain "identification" with that person, something to which I alluded when speaking of affinity. And such identification is a primordial effect of love, which makes it possible to understand our friends. Carlos Cardona expresses it in this way: "Only love permits a true knowledge of someone: the intelligence, the *intus legere*, to read inside; insofar as love identifies me with the other, puts me in his place, which is precisely what originates 'understanding,' a knowledge of someone that is exhaustive or total."[6] These words eliminate any impression that understanding is a question of technique, because its origin is in the heart of man and in his will, that is to say, in love, sensible and rational love, which attracts us toward our friends and identifies us with them, in order to thus know them *from within, that is, to understand them*.

Listening in Order to Understand

One thing that is necessary in order to understand people is to listen to them. This is something that seems obvious and is often taken for

---

6. Carlos Cardona, *Metafísica del bien y del mal*, (Pamplona: EUNSA, 1987), p. 117.

granted but not practiced in any depth. We can listen with other intentions: in order to answer the matter being presented, to give some advice, to carry out a particular action. In these cases, the message received is usually not the most important thing but a simple means for what we are trying to accomplish through it. The result is that we do not listen sufficiently. In contrast to this, when we listen *in order to understand*, the important thing is in the message itself and in the one who is bringing us that message, because that is where our intention is centered.

We have *to learn to listen*. A lot of effort is invested in learning to speak, to read, and to write—not, however in learning to listen. Listening is often taken for granted, and that is a grave mistake. To know how to listen is an art and cannot be reduced to something just for the ears. We listen with every part of our being: *with our eyes*, to capture the body language, which often transmits more content than the words themselves—a gesture, an expression of joy, or a simple presence can say more than many verbal explanations—*with our understanding*, to capture the reasons for what has been expressed and its relation with the person who expressed it; *with our hearts*, to participate in the sentiments of the other person and understand what that individual feels, since, according to the well-known phrase of Pascal, *The heart has its reasons that reason does not understand*. To listen is a task that requires effort and patience if we are really disposed to put ourselves in the footsteps of others, in order to thus understand them. When there is true friendship, friends like to listen to each other—because of the interest that they have in each other and because of the affinity that unites them. Thus they can be together, in a continual listening, where time quite often goes by without notice.

Inspiring Confidence

Another condition for understanding people is *that they show themselves to us as they are*—and not through appearances or lack of straightforwardness—which is greatly facilitated if we are capable of *inspiring trust*. When people meet someone in whom they feel confidence, they will act spontaneously, with naturalness and simplicity. This notably favors the process of becoming friends, and once it exists, it is reaffirmed by that way of acting.

What is it that makes us feel trust toward another person; what is the key to inspiring that trust? The basic principal is rooted in integrity of life, in authenticity, in consistency, in being *what I am and should be.*[7] This makes it likely that others trust in us by discovering a consistent way of acting that corresponds with our way of being. They know, among other things, that they are always understood and receive a positive response to their needs, since these are demands of the integral life of a person. Nor does this refer to a technique for inspiring trust, but on the contrary, the trust is inspired without directly trying to do so. Instead it is a result of going to the root of things, which is a way of being and of living authentically. If true friends have complete confidence in each other, it is because each one counts on the underpinnings of an upright and consistent life, which makes it possible for others to have no doubt of the friendship.

Being Understood

Since friendship is reciprocal—the friend is a friend for the friend—understanding between friends should also be mutual, which demands

---

7. See Francisco Ugarte, *En busca de la realidad*, (Madrid: Rialp, 2006), pp. 20–26.

not only an effort to understand our friends but also the disposition to facilitate that our friends understand us. How can this be facilitated? This is a matter of our friends *putting themselves in our place*, as a fundamental condition for understanding us. They will attain this if we are capable of transmitting what is within us—our feelings, our convictions, all that constitutes the interior world that is like a fountain from which all of our behavior comes. The content of that intimate core is made up of our emotional (or affective) and our rational lives as seen at that moment.

As I've said, the process of putting oneself in the place of the other emotionally has been called *empathy*, which consists in *feeling within,* in *entering into the others,* and in *succeeding in having the others enter into us*. Well, in making our friends participate in our feelings, we are permitting them to feel what we feel and in that way understand us. When this happens in a reciprocal way, a current of communication is established which can progressively strengthen our mutual understandings and thereby our friendships. Here we see clearly how "affective affinity" favors understanding.

The same thing occurs on the intellectual level if we are capable of opening ourselves and communicating to our friends what we think, our ideas, and our ways of seeing things, trying to make sense of all this. In doing so, we offer them the possibility of knowing us deeply, in such a way that if we, too, have had access to them on the same level, our friendships will acquire richness and solidity, permanence and stability, although we might disagree on many points.

We are now in a position to consider the third element of friendship. In speaking of affective affinity, I concluded that the communication of feelings is like the lubricant that makes it possible for the motor to function. Now I can add that understanding reinforces the lubrication in the relationship of friendship, but I now repeat the question: What good is the lubricant if the motor lacks some pieces ? The pieces are the objective content of the relationship that, as we shall see, is made up of *common interests*.

4.

Common Interests

f it is true that the step from companionship to friendship ordinarily begins with liking or empathy between the persons, by the affinity that they experience at the level of feelings, then it is also true that in some cases, the point of departure from companionship and the beginning of friendship can be found in another kind of affinity that might be called objective. This affinity consists in sharing some *common interest* with another person. The interest might be very varied—perhaps some sport, an artistic activity, or an intellectual subject—that we each like to share, giving rise to a relationship which can gradually develop into friendship.

In this case as well, the difference from companionship is clear, since the interest in question is not shared equally with other companions, and therefore, the relationship that develops is not shared equally with our other companions and has a certain character of exclusivity. "Friendship arises outside of mere companionship when two or more companions discover that they have certain ideas or interests in common, or simply some tastes that the others do not share and that until that moment each one thought was his own proper treasure, or his cross. The typical expression for the beginning of a friendship might be something like: 'what, you too? I thought I was the only one.'"[1]

The affinity that generates in this case has an *objective* character, because we and the other person feel ourselves drawn by the same object, which comes to be the point of meeting between us. It is not yet a matter of two individuals relating based on a single affective (emotional) attraction—but that of a relationship with a content that transcends us, since the common interest exists outside of us. Movies, the opera, technology, football, or culture, for example, could be that object, the point

---

1. Lewis, *The Four Loves*.

of meeting between we who feel ourselves attracted by it.

The difference from companionship is very clear. As companions, the basis of a relationship is an activity that we casually share, but from this, a deeper common interest arises that we don't share with the majority of our companions. The common interest is something objective, but in the sharing of it, we acquire a character of linkage between us that develops into a different relationship—into friendship. C.S. Lewis explains it as follows: "The Companionship was between people who were doing something together—hunting, studying, painting, or what you will. The Friends will still be doing something together, but something more inward, less widely shared and less easily defined; still hunters, but of some immaterial quarry; still collaborating, but in some work the world does not, or not yet, take account of; still travelling companions, but on a different kind of journey.[2]

To illustrate the function of common interests in the relationship of friendship, a helpful example is the contrast between two persons

2. Lewis, *The Four Loves*, p. 66.

who love each other as a couple, with a character of exclusiveness, and friends, whose immediate attention is focused on something external to them, but which is the object of their interest. "Lovers are normally face to face, absorbed in each other; friends, side by side, [are] absorbed in some common interest."[3]

When there are common interests, communication flows easily and the relationship is enriched. Since most people like to speak about a matter that draws our attention, there is an interchange of points of view and a sharing of experiences. If the sphere of association is a particular activity, such as a sport or the enjoyment of music, we seek occasions to enjoy this together. In short, there appears here—as in the case of "subjective affinity—an inclination for mutual closeness, accompaniment, and seeing each other frequently, although in this case, we are moved initially by the object of common interest. Getting together is also, for this reason, proper to friends in a double sense. Our common interests incline us to get together, and getting together allows us to share our interests.

---

3. Lewis, *The Four Loves*.

Diversity and Complementarity

We have to take into account that affinity at this objective level does not necessarily consist in friends seeing things in the same way, nor in being in accord with the solutions offered for problems, but in coinciding in our interest for the same subjects. For example, the common point of two friends might be in the field of digital technology, although each of them has his or her preferences as to the best programs. Or, if it is a matter of a love of classical music, both will agree on the beauty that it contains, although one might consider Mozart as the best composer ever while the other is convinced that Bach is insuperable.

Such differences in views on the same subject, which is important and interesting for both, can even favor the friendship, increasing the possibilities of mutually enriching one another by their different contributions. In other words, the affinity of common interests can be complementary and favored by the diversity of their outlooks. The interest of two friends can be centered on the economy, although they do not agree on the best system for a particular country, which leads them to exchange impressions and enrich each other's point of view. They may never reach an agreement, but they continue their passionate conversations on the subject, which fills many hours when they are together. It is most probable that their friendship will be strengthened by their mutual openness to dialogue.

The Weakness of Objective Affinity

Common interests are, let us say, the pieces of the motor that make up the content of the relationship of friendship. Nevertheless, now we have to emphasize the importance of the lubricant—the affective affinity or likableness—so that the motor functions, so that there is a communication of feelings and the relationship acquires or maintains its personal character. It may happen, for example, that a group of scientists work together in fields that they are passionately interested in for years, but they never transcend the relationship of companionship. Instead, they remain exclusively on the objective level of their interests, without entering into what is personal about each other. It is precisely here that the *weakness* of objective affinity is rooted; it does not necessarily produce a *personal* or intimate relationship between those who are communicating. There-fore, it requires the complement of mutual liking (*simpatía*) and the communication of feelings in order for it to be converted into friendship.

In contrast, both with the scientists just mentioned, as with those who bond exclusively through affective affinity (mutual liking), St. Augustine gives us his idea of his relationship with his friends, and his description seems to include both elements, common interests and shared feelings: "All kinds of things rejoiced my soul in their company—to talk and laugh and do each other kindnesses; read pleasant books together, pass from lightest jesting to talk of the deepest things and back again; dif-fer without rancor, as a man might differ with himself, and when most rarely dissension arose find our normal agreement all the sweeter for it; teach each other or learn from each other; be impatient for the return of the absent, and welcome them with joy on their homecoming; these and such like things, proceeding from our hearts as we gave affection and received it back, and shown by face, by voice, by the eyes, and a thousand other pleasing ways, kindled a flame which fused our very souls and of many made us one."[4]

In this description, there appear some elements that are shared feelings—laughing, amusing themselves, experiencing pain and joy—and others—conversing, arguing, and reading books—that pertain to their common interests.

I should now point out that not only does affective affinity favor the *personal* character of the relationship of friendship but also the individuals' common interests, since through those interests, each discovers the other person and knows him or her better—and they understand and like each other. In this way, the objective affinity is also converted into a bond of unity between the people thus connected. Unlike the scientists who consider their subjects in a neutral and objective manner, without involving themselves, the individuals now deal with the questions of common interest, while allowing their own personalities to be seen and permitting each of those involved to capture the way of thinking and the way of being of the other, who

4. Augustine of Hippo, *Confessions*, Second Edition, trans. F.J. Sheed, ed. Michael P. Foley, (Indianapolis: Hackett, 2006), IV, 8, 13, pp. 62–63.

in turn has a proper disposition to receive that knowledge. In this way, the common interests have an influence on the *personal* character of the friendship.

Quantity and Quality of Interests

With regard to the fundamental role that common interests play in the process of friendship, I should point out that the greater the richness contained in those interests, the stronger and more profound will be the bond between the friends. The richness of the interests refers both to the quantitative and the qualitative aspects; in both cases, it is a matter, logically, of good interests in the sense of those that favor the improvement of the persons. If there are many points of common interest, the relationship will be easier and more entertaining because of this variety; if the content of those interests both has quality and is deep—including, for example, human values: intellectual, artistic, or spiritual—the union between the persons will be fuller and more personal.

From this we can derive a consequence. The *capacity to make friends*, given affective affinity and understanding, depends on the interests that we have—or our capacity for acquiring them—both in number and in quality. The number of interests favors the quantity of friends. When we have more interests, there is greater facility to coincide with a greater number of persons and establish bonds of friendship. The quality of the interests favors the quality of the friendship: the greater the richness of those interests, the better friends we can make. It is not the same, for example, to coincide with someone exclusively in our interest in a sport as to share an interest in culture, human problems, or religious questions. And as the possibility of increasing the scope and content of our interests depends on us, we can say that the possibility of increasing our personal capacity for making friends is in our own hands.

To conclude this section, let us ask if the elements analyzed up to this point—affective affinity, understanding, and common interests—are enough for friendship to exist in a complete sense. We have seen that, when those conditions exist in the relationship, not only do we experience the inclination to be together, but, in addition, we find that being together is much more pleasant and enriching. Personal closeness, understanding, and common interests certainly establish a clear difference from what happens when the persons involved are only in a relationship of companionship. Now the relationship is more *personal*, because of the level of communication of feelings they have attained and by their mutual knowledge of each other. At the same time, they possess a richer *content*, due to the common interests that have arisen. For these reasons, we can already speak of friendship, although strictly speaking, we must say that we are now on the *threshold* of friendship, as we will see in the following pages in analyzing the fourth and final element of the friendly relationship.

5.

Interest in Our Friends

The elements that have appeared up until now, in the origin and process of friendship between two or more persons, are reciprocal affection, understanding, and common interests. According to this analysis, the human will, with its proper act which is to *love*, has intervened, especially in the third of the elements mentioned: an object of interest, when it attracts the will and arouses an act of love. For example, if someone is interested in human rights, he will decide to study them because he wants to know their content, their basis, their application to concrete cases, and so on, and such a decision is an act of the will. In the same way, my will might be attracted, not by some object of common interest, but by the person with whom I am interacting, that is, by the friend. In what does this "willed" liking consist—distinct from the sensible or affective inclination—that has for its object a human person? The response to this question leads us into the fourth element necessary for friendship.

The Intervention of the Will

The act of liking in its fullest sense is called loving and, according to Aristotle and St. Thomas Aquinas, to love means to desire for another person all that is considered good, but not for one's own benefit, but for that of the other.[1] This is a desire that has to be translated into deeds, that is to say, into a decision to use all the means within our reach to help others to better themselves and to attain the maximum good of which they are capable. For that reason, Tomás Melendo recalls that "genuine human love is essentially constituted by an act of the will, and without the active intervention of the will, in no sense can one speak of love as good will or love as friendship among men."[2]

---

1. See Aristotle, *Rhetoric*, 2, 4, 80b, and Thomas Aquinas, *Summa Theologica* 1–2, q. 26.

2. Tomás Melendo, *Ocho lecciones sobre el amor humano*, (Madrid: Ediciones Rialp, 2002), p. 81.

This act of the will implies our *choice* of a person—of a friend—from which, at the same time, there arises a commitment to seek that person's real, objective good. This often requires the renunciation of our own personal tastes and interests. It is for *each of us*, in our totality, to choose whom we love in and for ourselves and not because of some partial qualities. Those who say they are someone's friend for the material or financial benefit that they derive from that relationship evidently have not understood what friendship is. The same thing can be thought of those who are not disposed to accept their friends as they are, with their defects and qualities, or who are not capable of helping the friends to overcome them.

When our choice is authentic, the person of our friend is situated at the center of the relationship, that is, that person becomes the *principal content*, above those common interests that up until then occupied first place. This leap is transcendental for what it implies about the *personal* character of the relationship. The friend interests us more than those things that had been occupying our attention, our time, our efforts because we were passionate about them! Now the interest in our friend extends to everything that is part of that person's life. For this reason, we want to know our friends better, penetrate into their interiority, and discover their ideals and convictions in order to be able to share all that is theirs.

In a natural and spontaneous movement toward friendship, the step of choosing a friend usually takes place almost unconsciously, because it is the logical end of an ascending and continuous path, when other factors are favorable. "As a general rule, we can say that the more common factors there are between two people, the easier it is for them to unite through bonds of friendship, of love. Those elements, those shared bonds, can be of many different types: from attractions of character to the fact of exercising the same profession, belonging to the same political, sports, or religious group, living in the same neighborhood, being related by blood, etc. All of this, as we have said, is like a first impulse, that, from the psychological point of view, provokes or at least facilitates the beginnings of love and friendship."[3]

But it does not always happen this way. For example, the choice of a friend may occur

---

3. Melendo, *Ocho lecciones sobre el amor humano*, p. 60.

without being preceded by any affective affinity, by understanding, or by common interests. It is then as a consequence of this choice that the lacking elements appear later. When we make the decision to love people who do not appeal to us, our disposition toward those people changes; we start to discover their qualities, we begin to value them, and often the final result is that the original antipathy turns into liking. Or if we did not understand them originally, the changes of perspective and of dispositions derived from that decision lead to our understanding them and accepting them without any great difficulty. Something similar may occur with common interests, which begin to flourish after choosing to make friends with specific people. Let us go more deeply into these ideas, specifically in regard to the influence that the choice of the people has on our common interests and on their affective affinity (not including the influence on understanding, because that is already implicit in the development of the second element of friendship).

The Influence of the Choice of People as Friends on Their Common Interests

After the choice of a person, are common interests really relegated to a second place, losing their importance in the relationship of friendship? The answer is no because even though those interests cease to be the principal content of the relationship and a way of getting closer to our friends, it does not mean that they disappear, but the contrary. Now we are even more drawn toward those interests because they form part of the person we've chosen, part of that person's identity. Our taste for painting is greater when it forms part of the interests of our friend. This is a matter of a qualitative or intensive increase.

In addition, the scope of common interests also grows extensively, as a consequence of the choice of a friend. As the friendship progresses, we become interested in pursuits of that friend, pursuits we had been indifferent to previously. For example, we who had been indifferent to literature now begin to like it because our friend has passed on his or her interest in it. The intervention of the will, which affects our friend, is thereby enriched by the influence of our common interests. What previously interested us now interests us more, and what did not interest us, now begins to be interesting, and through this our friendships are notably increased.

The Influence of a Choice of this Person on Our Affective Affinity

And how does this choice affect our liking for the persons we choose? Before answering this question, it is worth noting the primacy of the intervention of the will over emotional affinity, without lessening the value of this affective affinity, which has already been emphasized. St. John Paul II said that "sympathy is not by any means the whole of love, any more than excitement and emotion are the whole of a human being's inner life—it is only one element among others. The most profound, by far the most important element is the will, in which the power to create love in a human being and between people is vested." And he added: "For in friendship—and here it is unlike mere sympathy—the decisive part is played by the will."[4]

---

4. Karol Wojtyla, *Love and Responsibility*, trans. H.T. Willetts (New York: Farrar, Straus and Giroux, 1981), p. 90.

With our choice of a person, the relationship acquires a more solid support than that provided by mere liking, for the simple reason that the will is more consistent than the emotions as a bond of unity, since the acts that derive from the will can enjoy greater permanence and stability. The feelings on the other hand easily vary; they suffer alterations that often escape personal control, which means that they offer few guarantees of stability in the relationship if it is based solely on them. This perhaps can be seen with special clarity in marriages. When a couple have united for purely sentimental reasons, once those feelings change and acquire negative tones such as anger, jealousy, and so forth, the relationship is shipwrecked. On the other hand, if the relationship is supported by the decision of the will to seek the good of the other person, no matter what happens, those sentimental variations are overcome and the marriage goes ahead. Gustave Thibon explains this with an example: "I often cite a phrase of Bismarck . . . on writing to his young wife, since she, a timid creature, had not accompanied him in all the vicissitudes of his brilliant career. She had written: 'I forget that I am a country girl, among your princesses and your ambassadors.' He answered, 'Do you forget that

I married you in order to love you?' This phrase
seems definitive to me. Not a simple 'because I
loved you,' but 'in order to love you,' which means
to drop anchor in the future. Separating an eter-
nal reality from the fleeting emotions of the feelings and of the imagination."[5]

Although I do not share the basic anthropology of Erich Fromm, it might be useful
here to cite some words of his that might seem
surprising, because of their coinciding with the
Christian outlook, and which clearly express
the idea that I am trying to present.

> "Love should be essentially an act of will, of
> decision to commit my life completely to
> that of one other person. This is, indeed, the
> rationale behind the idea of the insolubility of
> marriage. . . . In contemporary Western cul-
> ture this idea appears altogether false. Love is
> supposed to be the outcome of a spontaneous,
> emotional reaction, of suddenly being gripped
> by an irresistible feeling. . . . One neglects
> to see an important factor in erotic love, that
> of *will*. To love somebody is not just a strong
> feeling—it is a decision, it is a judgment, it is a

---

5. Gustave Thibon, *Entre el amor y la muerte* (Madrid: Rialp, 1997),
pp. 59–60.

promise. If love were only a feeling, there would be no basis for the promise to love each other forever. A feeling comes and it may go. How can I judge that it will stay forever, when my act does not involve judgment and decision?"[6]

The same occurs in relationships between friends. How many times have friendships that seemed invulnerable ended due to small differences that generated emotional reactions that they were not able to overcome? Actually, these were not true friendships, because there was no consciousness of a will capable of maintaining the relationship, beyond those sentimental reactions. When what we seek is the good of the friend, there is a forgetfulness of self and those personal differences lose their importance. We will speak clearly, rectify what is necessary, forgive, or ask forgiveness,[7] and thus the friendship is even strengthened. All of this is thanks to the predominance of our will over our feelings.

Now we can answer the question that was asked just paragraphs earlier: "How does this choice affect our liking for the persons we

---

6. Erich Fromm, *The Art of Loving*, (New York: Continuum, 2008), pp. 50–51.

7. See Ugarte, *From Resentment to Forgiveness*.

choose?" The choice of the person, in addition to strengthening the relationship of friendship, increases the affective affinity, the liking between the friends, for three reasons.

- First, because the choice of the person protects the relationship in time of weakness, the relationship is stable.

- Second, because the choice includes the entire person, with both good qualities and defects, it ordinarily produces a positive feeling toward the friend and increases the liking that arises spontaneously from *simpatia*, which proceeds from certain qualities and not from the totality of the person. The same positive feeling occurs in the person who is aware of being the object of that choice. Even more, when we do not feel a natural attraction for a person and suddenly discover that the person is sincerely interested in us, our feelings can change radically. "Meditate on this carefully and act accordingly: people who think you are unpleasant will stop thinking that when they realize that you *really* love them. It is up to you."[8]

---

8. Escrivá, *Furrow*, no. 734.

- Third, it guarantees the rectitude (uprightness) of our feelings if we are seeking the good for our friends. Feelings, when they lack the direction of the will, easily become egocentric because they seek self-satisfaction. In contrast, when love based on the will is solid, we seek the good of the other as an "other," and our feelings put themselves at the service of this end. As Cicero said in regard to bad moments, one tries "to strive with all his might to arouse his friend's prostrate soul and lead it to a livelier hope and into a better train of thought."[9]

This can open new horizons to any of us who desire to increase our number of friends, because clearly, the possibilities for friendship are not reduced to the cases in which there exists, spontaneously and from the beginning, a liking for others. The starting point can be a personal decision, that is to say a choice of someone whom we wish to make a friend. Something similar can be said for someone who wishes to deepen a friendship already begun or who wishes to keep alive a friendship through the passage of time, for

---

9. Cicero, *De Amicitia*, no. 59.

example, between spouses, between parents and children, and the like: the will can be the motor which continually enriches the process.

Reciprocity and Number of Friends

Of course, to have a friendship, it is not enough for someone to decide on this unilaterally. Although this has been implicit in all that I have been saying, it is worthwhile stressing that friendship, independent of the process that it follows, requires reciprocity: "A certain mutual love is requisite, since friendship is between friend and friend."[10] When correspondence is lacking, friendship does not exist. As Carlos Llano points out, "Without reciprocity one cannot speak of friendship in the strict sense. *Reciprocity* is a Latin-based word that is very expressive, we might almost say metaphoric, of the relationship of friendship, which is nourished by a certain coming and going, giving and receiving, bringing and taking. Literally it comes from the word for the ebb and flow that one finds in the sea."[11]

---

10. Aquinas, *Summa Theologica*, 2–2, q. 23, a.1.

11. Carlos Llano, *La amistad en la empresa*, (Mexico City, México: Fondo de Cultura Económica e IPADE, 2007), p. 91.

For this reason, an unmistakable result of authentic friendship is that we improve and overcome our defects continually through the help that we provide one another. As friends, we offer to one another the best of ourselves, that which most improves us. And we have to take into account that "the intention of making one's friend better has to adopt at times the form of correcting him. We have to learn how to correct if we want to be better friends and have better friends. It would be a shame if we were to fail to make a needed correction because we would be *good* friends of friends who are not *good*, and thus conforming with them in such a way that our *good* friendship becomes a falsehood."[12]

Finally, it is good to note that, although friendship is based on an act of choice, which is selective, it should not be exclusive. The more friends that we have—within the limits imposed by our own situations in life—the greater will be the personal enrichment and the possibilities of helping others. It would be a mistake to consider it otherwise, because then we would have to conclude that an ideal friendship exists only when there are just two people involved.

---

12. Llano, *La amistad en la empresa*, p. 224.

Two, far from being the necessary number for Friendship, is not even the best. . . . Lamb says somewhere that if, of three friends (A, B, and C), A should die, then B loses not only A, but "A's part in C," while C loses not only A but "A's part in B." In each of my friends there is something that only some other friend can fully bring out. By myself I am not large enough to call the whole man into activity; I want other lights than my own to show all his facets. Now that Charles is dead, I shall never again see Ronald's reaction to a specifically Caroline [that is, pertaining to Charles] joke. Far from having more of Ronald, having him "to myself" now that Charles is away, I have less of Ronald.[13]

The Spanish writer, Andrés Vázquez de Prada, responds with a suggestive metaphor to the question of the number of friends one person should have.

We know that the heart has its muscles which operate in an alternating rhythm of systole and diastole, that is of compression and expansion. That motor regulates the velocity and volume of the circulation of blood. A continued opening

---

13. C.S. Lewis, *The Four Loves*, p. 61.

of the valves would freeze the circulation. A sustained closure would paralyze the circulation and function of the blood. Well, this is how the heart works in friendship. A prudent number of friends keeps a person going and enriches him. Too many bleed him and if they are very few, he stagnates. There are those who by nature have a greater capacity for retaining friendships, but it is good for all of us to gradually increase our cardiac volume."[14]

The Greatest Good for One's Friend

If it is proper to friendship to wish the best for our friends; it is important to ask ourselves what is the greatest good that we can give to someone for whom we desire the best. We can say that, in each case, it depends on the recipient, for the circumstances and the needs of each person are different. We should note that it also depends on what those who want to do what is good really have to offer, since people can't give what they do not have, or in positive terms, we all

---

14. Andrés Vázquez de Prada, *Estudio sobre la Amistad*, (Madrid: Rialp, 1975), p. 163.

give what our capacities permit, according to the values that each of us possesses.

However, we can at the same time say, from a perspective of faith, that the greatest good that any of us can objectively possess is God himself, whose presence in our lives is the principal source of our present and future happiness. And as far as the receivers are concerned, whether they believe in God or whether they have put him inside a parenthesis, the greatest good that we can do for those friends, consistent with this perspective, would be to help them to increase or discover that presence of God, which will also make them happy. It is significant that Jesus explained why he called his disciples his friends: "I have called you friends, for all that I have heard from my Father I have made known to you" (Jn. 15:15).

It may certainly happen that some who try to bring a person closer to God will not succeed because there is lacking a disposition to receive that aid and the attempt is interpreted as an intrusion into one's private life. Nevertheless, this usually doesn't happen when there is true friendship, due to all that has been said earlier about relationships between friends. In the worst of cases, the target person does not accept what his or her friend offers but remains open to the possibility of accepting it in the future. Meanwhile, if the individual does accept it, that person has gained the most important thing, thanks precisely to the friendship with which it was offered. Thus we can understand the conclusion of St. Josemaría. "Friendship is a treasure, that we have to esteem in its great human value as a means of bringing souls to God."[15]

To Sum Up

It seems helpful to emphasize, finally, the interdependence that the four elements of friendship have with one another: affective affinity, understanding, common interests, and the choice of the person. None of these is sufficient to give us friendship, and, at the same time, each ends up being indispensable, although with varying degrees of importance.

Let's look at this.

1a) Personal liking (*simpatía*) without understanding is unstable because the moment that a contrary feeling arises in the relationship, there is usually no capacity to accept and channel it.

---

15. Josemaría Escrivá, Letter of March 11, 1940.

1b) Affective affinity (emotional bonding) without common interests leads to a relationship empty of content that either disappears or becomes deformed.

1c) Subjective affinity (signs of friendship), without the choice of the will, can be unstable or partial and end up in egoism.

2a) Understanding without affective affinity will always be incomplete, since it lacks empathy.

2b) Understanding without common interests can also exist, but at a superficial level, because there is a lack of material for understanding the other person deeply.

2c) Understanding without the choice of the person is insufficient because it lacks the generosity required to put ourselves in the place of the other and thus understand him or her.

3a) Common interests without subjective affinity are insufficient for the relationship to turn into friendship, because the relationship does not get to the personal level and remains at the level of companionship, where there is simply a sharing of a common activity.

3b) Common interests without understanding between the persons involved can polarize the relationship as soon as there are differences of opinion.

3c) Common interests without the choice of the person are insufficient because of the lack of a personal character, essential to friendship. The shared interests will tend to have greater importance than the friend as such.

4a) If the choice of the person lacks affective affinity, the relationship will not be able to flow. However, this can be overcome if, with time and as a consequence of the interest in the other, *simpatía* blossoms and the friendship firms up.

4b) If the option of the person does not include understanding, there cannot be identification. However, if the choice is unwavering, it will end up breaking down the resistance to understanding the other, putting oneself in that person's shoes.

4c) If the choice of the other person lacks common interests, the relationship will lead to boredom and will collapse. It may be, however, that as a consequence of the choice, some common interests that did not exist in the beginning will slowly be generated, in which case the relationship will turn into friendship.

From all of this one can conclude that, while liking (*simpatía*), understanding, and common interests are indispensable for friendship, the most important element is interest in our friends, which demands a choice on the part of the will. This choice considerably strengthens the other elements, giving them richness and consistency, and even bringing them forth if any of them is lacking.

Conclusion

I have now shown the great value of friendship as a component of human life. We men and women are complementary beings; we are not sufficient by ourselves. We need others to make up for our insufficiency. Friends are the natural complement to overcome those limitations. From them we receive affection, understanding, and help. With them we share what we possess, in a permanent process of reciprocal enrichment. To them we give the best of ourselves so that they attain their plenitude.

As friends, we sympathize with each other; we communicate our feelings. We suffer together; we rejoice together. We identify with each other strongly through the affection that unites us, and we support each other unconditionally. We enjoy being together, sometimes exchanging impressions in passionate conversations; at other times, spending unforgettable hours together, where words are not even needed. This comradeship flows spontaneously, because of our identification of feelings, because of the emotional harmony that exists in true friendship.

As friends, we understand each other because we are fond of each other. We know our true friends deeply. We understand why they react in one way or another, why they adopt certain attitudes at particular moments, and why they see the problems that affect them in those ways. As true friends, we enter into the interior of our friends to grasp them from within, both emotionally and intellectually, to feel what they feel—empathy—and to understand their concepts—their standards—with the particular vision that derives therefrom. For this, we have to listen and inspire confidence. We also have to let ourselves be known, to communicate feelings and ideas, so that our friends and we understand one another—and thus the reciprocity proper to all true friendships is established.

As friends, we have common interests that serve as a bond of union. Those interests have a certain character of exclusivity, insofar as they are not shared, in the same way, with everyone else. Just for this reason, the relationship between us as friends becomes different: We can only speak with each other about certain subjects; only with each other can we discuss particular ideas; only with each other can we exchange certain points of view, which would be of no interest to others. In that exchange, we complement and enrich each other. Also, as we project ourselves into that which we share, our knowledge of each other grows and increases our friendship. As true friends, we come to have many common interests, among which some have a greater content and quality, which enriches our relationship.

As friends, we are really fond of each other; we are interested in each other, and each of us desires the good of the other. We accept each other as we are, with our qualities and defects. We help each other to improve, to grow as human beings. Our response is unconditional in the face of any need. As friends, we commit ourselves to do whatever we can to see to it that our friends are happy, that they reach the plenitude to which they are called. In the spiritual terrain, if we have faith, we see to it that our friends meet and unite themselves with God, the greatest good that we can offer to them. The decision to seek the good of our friend is total, absolute, and unconditional.

Works Cited

Aesop. "The Two Fellows and the Bear." *Aesop's Fables,* retold by Joseph Jacobs, 1902. This text is in the public domain.

Aquinas, Thomas. *Summa Theologica.* Translated by Fathers of the English Dominican

Province. New York: Benziger Bros., 1948.

———. *Commentary on The Nicomachean Ethics.*

———. *Commentary on Saint Matthew's Gospel.*

Aristotle. *The Eudemian Ethics.* Translated by Brad Inwood and Raphael Woolf. New York: Cambridge University Press, 2013.

———. *Nicomachean Ethics.*

Augustine of Hippo. *Confessions.* Second Edition. Translated by F.J. Sheed, ed. Michael P. Foley. Indianapolis: Hackett, 2006, IV, 8, 13, pp. 62-63.

Bacon, Francis. "Of Friendship." *The Essays: Or Counsels, Civil and Moral.* New York: Oxford University Press, 1999.

Cabodevilla, Jose Maria. *El cielo en palabras terrenas.* Madrid: Paulinas, 1990.

Cardona, Carlos. *Metafísica del bien y del mal.* Pamplona: EUNSA, 1987.

Cicero, Marcus Tullius. On Old Age, On Friendship, and On Divination. Translated by W. A. Falconer. Cambridge, MA: Harvard University Press, 1923.

Covey, Stephen R. *The 7 Habits of Highly Effective People: Powerful Lessons in Personal Change.* New York: Simon & Schuster, 2004.

Demir, Meliksah *et al.* "I Matter to My Friend, Therefore I am Happy: Friendship, Mattering, and Happiness." *Journal of Happiness Studies 12,* no. 6, (2011).

Escrivá, Josemaría. *Furrow.* New York: Scepter, 2011.

Ferguson, Kitty. *Pythagoras: His Lives and the Legacy of a Rational Universe.* Electronic Edition: London: Icon Books, 2010; Print Edition: New York: Walker, 2008.

Fromm, Erich. *The Art of Loving.* New York: Continuum, 2008.

Goleman, Daniel. *Emotional Intelligence.* New York: Bantam, 1995.

Lewis, C. S. *The Four Loves.* New York: Harcourt Brace, 1960.

Llano, Carlos. *El Liderazgo Anamórfico.* Mexico City: IPADE, 1994.

———. *Humildad y liderazgo: ¿necesita el empresario ser humilde?* México City: Ediciones Ruz, 2004.

———. *La amistad en la empresa.* México City: Fondo de Cultura Económica and IPADE, 2007.

Malo, Antonio. *Antropología de la afectividad*. Pamplona: EUNSA, 2004.

Malraux, André. *Man's Hope*. Translated by Stuart Gilbert and Alastair Macdonald. New York: Random-House, 1938.

Marina, José Antonio. *El laberinto sentimental*. Barcelona: Anagrama, 1997.

Melendo, Tomás. *Ocho lecciones sobre el amor humano*. Madrid: Rialp, 1993.

Nazianzen, Gregory. "The Panegyric on S. Basil," in *Nicene and Post-Nicene Fathers, Second Series VII*. Translated by Charles Gordon Browne and James Edward Swallow. Edited by Philip Schaff and Rev. Henry Wallace. New York: Cosimo, 2007.

Ocáriz, Fernando. *Amar Con Obras: a Dios, y los hombres*. Madrid: Palabra, 1974.

Ortega y Gasset, José. *Obras completes II: El Espectador*. *Revista de Occidente*, 1946.

———. "Estudios sobre el amor." *Revista de Occidente*. Madrid: Alianza Editorial, 1981.

Pope Francis. Apostolic Exhortation *Evangelii Gaudium*. (November 2013).

Plutarch. *Moralia II*. Translated by Frank Cole Babbitt. Cambridge, MA: Harvard University Press, 1971.

Ramón y Cajal, Santiago. *Charlas de café: pensamientos, anécdotas y confidencias*. Madrid: Espasa-Calpe, 1966.

Rivarol, Antoine de. *Pensamientos y Rivarolianas*. Madrid: Editorial Periférica, 2006.

Sala, Felipe Jacinto. "La nube" in *Nuevas fábulas*. Barcelona: Librería de Juan y Antonio Bastinos, 1866.

Thibon, Gustave. *Entre el amor y la muerte.* Madrid: Rialp, 1997.

Ugarte, Francisco. *From Resentment to Forgiveness: A Gateway to Happiness.* New York: Scepter, 2008.

———. *En busca de la realidad.* Madrid: Rialp, 2006.

Vázquez de Prada, Andrés. *Estudio sobre la Amistad.* Madrid: Rialp, 1975.

von Hildebrand, Dietrich. *The Heart: An Analysis of Human and Divine Affectivity.* South Bend, IN: St. Augustine Press, 2007.

Wilde, Oscar. *The Soul of Man under Socialism.* New York: Max N. Maisel, 1915.

Wojtyla, Karol. *Love and Responsibility.* Translated by H. T. Willetts. New York: Farrar, Straus & Giroux, 1981.